Fitting In Is For Sardines

By
John Roedel

John Roedel

Fitting In Is For Sardines by John Roedel

Copyright © 2023, John Roedel All rights reserved. No portion of this book may be reproduced in any form without permission from the publisher, except as permitted by U.S. copyright law.

For permissions contact: johnroedel@gmail.com

Author Website: www.johnroedel.com

Cover photo by golden_designs1
www.fiverr.com/golden_designs1

ISBN: 9798852173317

printed in the USA

Fitting In Is For Sardines

Dedicated to Noah - thank you for teaching me how to live without apologies. You are a living masterclass for all of the world in the miracles that follow once we have the courage to embrace our story.

John Roedel

Prologue & Foreshadowing

I was 16 years old
and it was my turn
to share with my
circle of fellow
misfits

I had recently been invited
to take part in an
after school program
that I was told was
for "creative" kids

it was explained
to me by my parents
that this program
would be a fantastic experience
for me to help explore
and develop my "imagination"

at that point in my life
my imagination
was my best friend

so this seemed like
a wonderful match

in hindsight,
I probably should have seen
that it was all a ruse

the thing about me is,

I was born
into a family
of scientists
and deep thinkers
and academics

~ and I wasn't one of them

I was the intellectual
third wheel in a family
of four

instead of doing my algebra
I would scribble short stories about
dreaming coma patients and talking statues
on the back of my homework sheets

instead of memorizing historical facts,
I practiced my stand-up comedy
in the mirror that I would use the next
day at the high school lunch table

I wrote love letters and lyrics
when I should have been writing colleges

the older I was getting
the less I was relaying on
what I thought

~ I was all about *how I felt*

when it became clear
to me that I just didn't
care about maintaining
the whole love triangle between
myself, my heart, and my brain

I let my mind file for emancipation
~ so it left soo after without any fanfare

and packed
up my academic career
with it

which understandably
bothered my parents
who valued the educational system
the way a farmer values rain

my parents wanted
me to have a plan for my life

and I wanted life to be a constant
surprise party

John Roedel

Fitting In Is For Sardines 6

why worry about four years from now
when I had a sandwich in my hand right now?

who cares about the job market in a decade
when I could lay naked in the bathtub and listen
to Michael Stipe and R.E.M. sing about gardening at night?

my parents believed in concrete
and I believed in ocean-kissed sand

we were at an impasse

that is why they
"encouraged" me
to attend the after school
program for "creative" kids

I became suspicious
when I walked into
the first meeting
and discovered
that there were no
items that a "creative"
kid might use

there were no pencils
or paper
or paintbrushes
or instruments
or glue

there were just chairs
arranged in a circle

the other kids
who were at the
meeting had the same
look in their eyes
as I did

the look
of a person
who had
surrendered to
their heart

John Roedel

and the expense of
their brain

we were a collection
of kids who were bookended
with quotation marks
like they were our diagnoses

"emo"
"different"
"quiet"
"funny"
"weird"
"outsider"
"creative"
"trouble"
"unwell"

it was all code
for being kids who
were considered at risk

my allegiance to my
heart had become a liability
to me in the eyes of the adults

the meeting opened
with a song by Cyndi Lauper
played on a cheap boom box

"I can see your true colors..."

what they almost saw
was me vomit

within a few moments
it became clear to me
that we weren't there to
explore our creativity

we were there to be
evaluated to make
sure we weren't
on the highway to
self-harm

John Roedel

it was evident that
we were considered
kids who were in need of fixing

we were the boxes
of crumpled cereal
that gets shoved to
the back of a grocery shelf

the theme of the meeting
weren't as much about creativity
as it was explaining how we thought
that we had gotten broken

but I didn't feel broken
I just felt miscast
for the role, I had been given to play

I viewed my life as an unfolding
river

where behind every bend
there was another unexpected
valley to explore

how in the hell
was I going to
explain any of that?

31 years later - I still can't

we all sat in a circle
with our heads bowed
down waiting for our
turn to explain
our perceived brokenness

it was my turn
and I prayed for
an earthquake to swallow
the whole room up in one
gulp

"Why do you think you are struggling so much in school,"
my guidance counselor asked.

John Roedel

she wanted to see my true colors

I squirmed in my seat
and stared over her head
at the bright red exit sign
behind her

I said something like:
"I dunno"
and tried to hide within myself

"Think about it," she pressed

I couldn't think about it
as I had let my brain
float out of my skull
years ago like a bright
pink birthday balloon

I stared back at her
and simply said

"Because school sucks. Can I go now?"

With that answer I became
a teenage cliche
of disconnected surliness

I wish I had said something else
since it was the answer:
"Because school sucks. Can I go now?"
was the one that she
had been specifically trained to respond to

I fell right into the trap of her well-intended script
she then lectured me on the importance of my education
and how I needed to take advantage of all of the
opportunities in my life that I was blessed to have

and how I was letting down my parents
and what kind of job would I be able to get with that kind of attitude.
and..and...and...and...

I nodded along like I was absorbing
her well-intended pearls

John Roedel

when actually I was just
hiding in the panic room
in my heart

she was giving a passionate
monologue that I had heard all of my life

it was a speech likely called
"get your head out of the clouds"

the thing is I have always loved clouds

~ clouds are where the angels are
and possible UFOs
and the secrets of heaven

clouds are billowing and mysterious
and without form

which was exactly how
I wanted to live my life

~ formless
~ moving

a brand new creation
every five seconds

that's what I wanted to be
I wasn't interested in the answers to life

I was interested in the questions that had no answers

at the end of the only
meeting of "creative" kids
that I ever attended

I was given a piece of paper
that had a simple question on it

"Who do you want to be?"

I never filled out the paper
because I didn't know
what I wanted to be

John Roedel

I still don't
not really

if anything
I want to have a
heart made
of cotton candy

that's it

I want a heart
that's easy to pull apart
and to dissolve
away under the
the hot breath of
the present moment

I want to remove pieces of my confectionary
heart every day and place it in your hands
and wait for you to consume it
and wait for you to understand me

Who do I want to be now?
Understood.

I guess that's it.

    Can I go now?

John Roedel

#1

the only thing to say when
somebody tells you that
you've changed is:

"Thank you."

and maybe they have it wrong
maybe we are not changing at all

maybe we are just simply becoming
the person who I was created
to be

~ my love, it seems as if I'm always in a cocoon

over the past couple of years
people have told me that they
miss the old me

~ the funny me
the less-serious version of me

~ the safe me
the less-wandering version of me

I try to explain to them
that lately
my favorite places
have become thresholds

I have about four new seasons a week
but I'm the same planet

I'm constantly unfolding like a
blanket with no end

I'll try doing *this* and then
~ I'll try being *that* and then

I'll try *this on* and then

John Roedel

~ I'll try *a taste* of that

I may *write a poem* today
I'll *take some photos* tomorrow

and maybe I'll tell some
jokes on stage next week

and a decade from
now I'll be painting sunflowers

and each thing will be the most
important thing I've ever done

    ~I'm in a perpetual state of transition

I keep leaving home
as who I was and
returning as who I
need to be next

~ it's all such a skin-shedding
adventure of fresh starts and
unlimited resurrections

I don't want to be the exact same
person that I was when you
last saw me yesterday

too much has happened since then;

I've seen too much beauty
I've cried too many tears
I've sat with too many ghosts on park benches
I've put my toes in too many rivers
I've had my heart broken too many times
I've felt too many kisses

I've heard God singing to me from too many treetops to not be
transformed

I once met an angel that was sunbathing
in a garden who told me that

heaven looks like a thunderhead
draping itself over a Rocky Mountain valley

John Roedel

heaven is always billowing
heaven is ever rolling
heaven is constantly churning
heaven is relentlessly changing forms

heaven never looks the same
from one day to the next

heaven is constantly being reshaped by the
hands of the great Potter

because

it turns out that grace is a
whirling spectrum of
color

and heaven has to keep
changing its form in
order to keep up with it

heaven transforms
its camouflage of miracles
and magic every morning

and if that's good enough for heaven
then it's good enough for me

there is so much creation
taking place around us
for us not to join in
on the fun

so many new opportunities
so many new people
so many galaxies are being formed
so much ancient beauty is being rediscovered

with all of that going on
how can we have a new
beginning every single
time we breathe?

I believe epiphanies aren't
meant to randomly drip

John Roedel

Fitting In Is For Sardines 15

like a broken faucet

they're meant to flood
like a creating river

when somebody accuses you of changing

take it as a compliment and wonder
why they haven't

if a nebula can be given
permission to change forms
so can you

besides ~ maybe we aren't
changing anyway

maybe we are just becoming
who we were born to be
in the first place?

maybe we were born
to keep unfolding
like an endless map

and one last thing, my love,

don't let any of your seasons
become permanent
let them all pass through you

bloom red
change
bloom green
change
bloom rainbows

embrace each one as the wonder
that they are

you see,

our souls are made of moving
water

with bits of sunlight in it

John Roedel

we are all glowing ripples
passing through time
reflecting light off of water

don't fret, my love,

heaven is called to
reinvent itself daily

as are we

as are we
as are we

and I can't wait to
see how beautiful
you look the next
time I see you

radiating like
cathedral stained glass
under the glow of your
raw ever-changing

Authenticity

John Roedel

#2

**"SOMEDAY YOU WILL FIT IN
AND INSTANTLY REGRET IT"**

I used to carry this note
in my pockets wherever
I went as a warning to quit
comparing myself to others

I used to be so obsessed
with making my life
resemble everyone else's

eventually

~ after a lot of needless suffering I
discovered that my desire
to look normal was killing me

it was death by conformity

my love,

don't waste time
trying to fit in

remember that
in the entire history
of the cosmos

there will only be
one you

your life is a singular
event

you are the rarest
wonder the universe
will ever know

John Roedel

your life is a song that
will only be sung once

every breath you
take makes history

don't chase the fake
rainbow of comparison

you won't find
any gold there

because it turns out

that you are
already golden

my love,
be unashamedly

you you you you you

don't clone your life
own your life

John Roedel

#3

be so very
careful

when trying to fit
in

with everybody
else

~ because accidentally
someday

you just
might ~

stay fully wild,
star child

ride your watermelon
bike

wear your purple polka dot
pants

dream your dripping honeycomb
dreams ~

remain always untamed,
free spirit,

don't give up on what makes you
different

be the red
umbrella

be the horseshoe
nebula

John Roedel

be the dancing
fool

be the mismatched
socks

be the walking piece of rainbow shag
carpet ~

because because because

you weren't plucked from
nothingness

to simply fit
in

you were created to make us
gasp ~

seduce us with your
strangeness

wear your authenticity like
lingerie

quit pretending to be so
khaki

while you are covered in
so many watercolors ~

continue being weird my
beautiful weirdo

remember remember remember

fitting in is for sardines

John Roedel

#4

every morning I have a blind date
with my body

and as I do

a million questions
run through my head

who is this person
sitting across from
me in the mirror?

am I my own soulmate?

are the dreams in my he
and my thoughts in my head
perfect strangers?

how can I open my heart
to this imperfect human
who is staring back at me?

how can I learn to love
their wrinkles?

how can I build a
future with this person?
and every morning
during my blind date
with my own image

I remember the secret
to any great relationship

to is let them see you
as you really are

~ so, how do I see myself?

as a piece of cosmic art

John Roedel

Fitting In Is For Sardines 22

or as a half-shattered bowl?

maybe it's both things
at the same time

my love,

in order to feel at home
in your skin

you must learn to
be yourself
with yourself

and to see the beauty
in yourself
when you look at yourself

all first dates
are awkward

~so be patient with yourself

as you get to know the person
in the mirror

don't let them slip
through your fingers

because

~ they are the love of your life

John Roedel

#5

here is a story about you
that I heard from a gossiping angel
who was snacking on a strawberry
in the tree in my backyard this past summer

the angel said that

you used to soar
above the world

they said that

you were once surrounded
by so many miracles
that nobody could tell
where the wonder began and you ended

you were a swirl
of soaring grace

but one day *(a long while ago)*

a comet came roaring down
and the sky came apart all around you

and after being so wounded

you became grounded to gravity
and found yourself wounded and walking
in a foreign land

eventually, you were captured by those
who told you that flying was now
too dangerous

they said that
that you would enjoy
the safety of confinement

so, they put you in a cage

John Roedel

and clipped your wings

for "your own safety"

the angel went on to say that

for years you stared through
the iron bars and fantasized about
taking flight once more

~ to feel the great wind on your face
~ to be untethered to earthly things
~ to be able to flirt with heaven again

I heard that you dreamed
every night about being
able to reclaim your freedom

"but your freedom never came,"
the angel told me

and over time,
you fell into a deep despair

"I'll never leave this place," you repeated
to yourself over and over

The angel said that in your
most desperate hour
you even prayed for God to let
your heart to stop beating

so you could become a ghost
in order to feel yourself become
tangled up in a hot summer breeze

- *even if just for a second*

I heard that you prayed to Spirit
to allow your suffering to end

Even if that meant that you
would be swept up by oblivion

I began to weep as I listened to your story
because it sounded so familiar

John Roedel

Fitting In Is For Sardines 25

the angel reported somberly that
your prayers were never answered

and you resigned yourself
to being stuck in the cage forever

then the angel said that

during one winter night
 (not too long ago)
a moonbeam winked at you
through the gaps of your cage bars

and how overtaken you were
by the soft glow

and how you sang a psalm about
how lovely it all was

the moon heard you
And changed its hue from
white to lavender

and suddenly you remembered
something you were told when
you first hatched

your voice can
change the world
and that

there is no prison
that can hold your song

the angel said that even though
 they clipped your wings
 and put you in a cage

you let your voice grow feathers
and it slips out through the cage every
night to explore the world

every time you open
your mouth and sing
you escape the prison

John Roedel

that you thought you
would never leave

I heard that you learned
that you didn't need your
wings to be close to heaven

you just needed
to find your voice

and as the angel hugged me goodbye
she told me

that once you started singing
~ you never stopped

and that now you are surrounded
by so many miracles that nobody can
tell where the wonder begins and you end

you are still such a swirl
of soaring grace

oh, my love,

as the strawberry scented
angel rose up I shouted

*how I couldn't wait to hear
your song*

because

*maybe it will
help me find
the way out
of my own cage*

John Roedel

#6

if Creation had
waited for the
"perfect moment"

to explosively
kiss everything
into existence

this great adventure
we are all on would
have never started

was the Big Bang
God's first smooch?

was the Divine nervous
in the slightest
when it initially touched lips
with infinite possibility?

my love,

when I softly lay
my hand on
your cheek

I can feel it

~ the building
tension under your skin

I can feel it

~ the coming explosion
of your sacred purpose

that it created
a ripple that
is still turning nothingness
into miracle?

John Roedel

my love,

there is so much
swirling energy
inside of you

holding its breath
for you to
quit waiting

on the "perfect moment"
for you to release it

now
now is
now is the
now is the perfect
now is the perfect time

~ to set your life to blaze

my love,

I know how afraid
you are about what
will happen when you
finally unleash your power

you're worried that if you
allow all of that energy building up
inside of you to be unleashed

that you won't ever
ever be able to control
where the ripples that create
will go

you are scared that if
you allow yourself
to ignite like Genesis

it will change and
terraform our world

~ but that's exactly what

John Roedel

we are all hoping for

oh my love,

don't be afraid of your power

*you are the glowing
Angel of New Beginnings*

and I can hardly wait
to watch how you transform
everything under the sacred
fire of your reclaimed purpose

John Roedel

#7

Their gossip
Isn't your story

Their rumoring
Doesn't define who you are

You are the appraiser of
Your own self-worth

Remember, my love
You are a timeless masterpiece

John Roedel

#8

I used to wonder
why it seemed like my
heart hardened with every
year that passed?

I was mindlessly becoming a
thick fossil of judgments
and beliefs that people will someday
dig up long after was gone

and what will they find?

a person who was so stuck
in the amber of his own
need to be right about everything
that they stopped fighting to
explore the mystery of existence

a person who is suspended
in the moment in time
where they felt the most
self-righteous

a relic that was forever
entombed by their own
sticky pride

oh, my love,

I allowed myself to be seduced by
the cozy little cottage my narcissism
had built for me to spend the rest
of my days hiding inside of

it was a well-constructed hobble
that allowed me to become
a hermit whose only friend
would be my vanity

everything was easy

John Roedel

and the days passed quietly

then came the great earthquake
that rose up out of the mantle of the Earth
to rip straight through my
comfortable little home
of certainty and self-importance

it turns out that the jagged edges
I allowed to form around my heart
weren't designed to survive an apocalypse

and I was left with nothing
but the shattered remains of
my once comfortable selfish life

it was there in my desolation
that I decided I would never
build my home out of the granite
of my hardened thoughts and opinions

the next home I would live in
wouldn't have any doors or walls

it would be a place
where all things would come and go
with each passing breeze

it turns out that I traded
in my ego's comfy cottage for

a roaring wind tunnel

where each moment
is a wild gust of newness

where every grudge that
asks me to hold it
is taken away by moving air

where every judgment I used
to cling to is swept away
by blustering mercy

where all of my certainty I used
to hoard is stolen by the flurry

John Roedel

of mystery and wonder

and once I became an
open passage

my heart immediately
melted from a rock into
singing wind chime

because it turns out
that we aren't here to
become stationary fossils

we are here to become
a clambering hymn amid
the rushing gale of life

but first, we have to untether
ourselves from ego and our
addiction for controlling
our time on Earth

and let the wind
rush through us

and then we will hear it…

our song

and we won't ever become
a jaded rock ever again

because we will
be of the air

my love,

our egos make
for the worst retirement home

as the years pass
and our hair greys

let's live our time
together on the breeze

John Roedel

and I swear,

every single gusting day
that remains will give us a
brand new song to play

so, let the wind come steal
our hats and unravel our hair

because the adventure
into our wide-open heart

is going to be such a wild ride

John Roedel

#9

You be you
& I'll be me.

Let's not ever worry
about trying to be each other.

Turn the tables
on conformity.

Disturb the peace
with your originality.

We don't need
a world full of "them".

We need you.

Don't live somebody
else's life.

Your dreams.
Your passions.
Your expectations.
Not theirs.
Not mine.

Yours. Yours. Yours.

Get moving.
Time is growing short.

Be weird.
Be you.
Be original.

Go make some noise.
Go break some eggs.
Go knock down some ceilings.

Be unashamedly you

John Roedel

and once you do

your future tombstone is
going to need a lot
of room to explain what
came next.

#10

today is the day you
stop living somebody
else's life

isn't it so exhausting
acting like who they
want you to be?

haven't you noticed
how telling a story
that isn't your own
can suck the light
right out of you?

my love,

you may only get
one crack at this
adventure of living

so, today is the day you will scrape off
the grey paint they slathered
on the walls of your once unburdened heart

and make those who are
trying to co-opt your life to
gaze slack-jawed under the blazing
wallpaper that Creation wrapped
you in on your first day

it's time for them to see you in
all of your intended celestial
beauty and singular fire

today is the day you
stop being who the gatekeepers
expect you to be

John Roedel

and become the wild bloom
of Genesis that you were
imagined to be years ago

today
today
today

you will unfold
your petals

and join the buzzing
field of unafraid storytellers

John Roedel

#11

3:30 a.m. - *I've been up all night.*

And now I really can't sleep because I just learned that a group of butterflies is called a kaleidoscope.

I'm overwhelmed by that word:

                    kaleidoscope.

I close my eyes and imagine I'm walking through a thick forest. Every tree is filled with dozens of broken open chrysalis'.

I walk into a clearing.
I can see them now.

A swirl of fluttering colors.
A breathing wave of change agents.

The sky above me is now a billowing canvas
of dancing droplets of sacred paint.

The sound of ten thousand hovering wings
announce the end of winter.

The reign of the
smothering grey is over.

The season of dancing
rainbows has officially begun.

The kaleidoscope is growing
as more and more specks of
color rise up to join the festival.

The kaleidoscope is kissing
every dead back tree back to life.

I detect a hint
of maple in the air

John Roedel

and decide that it must be
what resurrection smells like.

The kaleidoscope of butterflies
is transforming the frozen foggy world
into a spinning prism of new life.

I open my eyes. It's now 4 a.m. I still can't sleep. How can I? I have a living kaleidoscope inside of me. They are kissing all my dead parts back to life. I can hear them fluttering when I hold my breath. I've never felt so warm. There are so many empty cocoons in me. I'm transforming. My skin is constantly shedding under a pulsing beat of rainbow light shards.

I'm a child of Spring

*and suddenly I can taste
maple syrup on my lips.*

John Roedel

#12

Dear ego, it's time for the big talk.
Better strap in.

I'm not here to tame this world.
I'm here to gently explore it.

to wander through its rolling hills,
to soak in the warmth of its summer sun,
to feel the cool mist of its autumn rain,
to experience the frostbite of its winter fangs,
to listen to the resurrection ballad of its spring bloom

I'm not here to control the world
I'm here to become overwhelmed by it.

I'm not here to own a river.
I'm here to surrender to the flow.

I know you want me to be more ambitious and turn my library into a trophy room - but I didn't carefully sneak under the velvet rope of existence to spend my time here on Earth using someone else's compass.

I came here to get lost in Creation's delicious backcountry.

I came here to get lost in the
tangled vines and ancient trees,
to feel the soft earth beneath my feet,
to drink in the wild scents of flowers and herbs

Let others pave every inch of everything. Let them turn a pocket supercomputer into their family. Let them buy front-row tickets to watch billionaires ride rockets.

There isn't enough time to waste doing any of that. In the days I have left, I'm here to follow butterflies into the wilderness that exists all around and all through me.

John Roedel

Oh, my dear ego, today, I ask for you to release me, so I can finally become a piece of driftwood on the moving holy water of the unfolding river.

In the time I have left, I'd like to trade in all of the safety I have been hoarding for the opportunity to hear mystery sing to me against canyon walls.

In the time I have left, I'd like to replace my worry about where I am going with my desire to just keep flowing.

Oh, dear ego, this is my clumsy way of thanking you for being in control for so long. You must be exhausted.

So, I'll take over from here. You better strap in because I'm taking us straight out into the boondocks of wonder.

Do you hear that drumming? That's my heart racing. You will get used to it. Like I said, you better strap in.

Because, my dear ego, it's all adventure from here on out.

John Roedel

#13

DIFFERENT IS NOT BROKEN

DIFFERENT IS BEAUTIFUL

John Roedel

#14

what you give
to the world

is who you are

we are not here
to hoard the light

we are here to reflect it

our souls don't
have pockets

everything we fought to gather
will one day slip through our
unclenched translucent hands

nobody will remember
how safe we were with
our gifts and heart

they will remember how
recklessly we gave of ourselves

we aren't here to
turn our lives into
a bank vault

we are here to be
a gateless park

oh, my love,

I wasted so many
years before I learned
that

we are not what we take
from this world

John Roedel

*we are defined by what we
give back to it*

#15

(an open poem to closed hearts)

when you hate
someone else

because they are
different than you

you are unknowingly hating on
the very Architect of Creation itself

~ to rage against a color
you have never seen before

because it's exotic
tincture offends
your orthodox eyes

suggests that you believe
the Divine Artist is worried
about what you think

did the first burst of
cosmic energy care
about its critics when
it began to paint life
across the constantly
unfolding canvas of
the known universe?

hell no

it just wildly created
this delicate masterpiece
of endless fire, orchestrated chaos
and a trillion or so wobbling worlds
like a Michelangelo made out of an
army of swarming angels

John Roedel

every inch of everything
that exists is a unique piece
of abstract splatter art

so, if the Divine was so
unrestrained when
it came to creating
the stretching forever
kingdom of stars

it would make sense
that God was even
more uninhibited when
it came to how we
were made

each of us are a wow sculpture of
unbridled never-seen-before genius

who are you
to decide how
The Everlasting Potter
molds their art?

get over your fear
of people who

look
live
pray
love
believe

differently than you do

because the more you hide
from what is foreign to you

the more you hide from
the miracle of this existence

you only get to ride this
skin and bone rollercoaster
for so long

quit closing your eyes

John Roedel

stare into the swirl

because that's where God's
most profound artwork is

hurry up
open your eyes

you're missing it

open your eyes
hurry up

and once you do
you will see it

the relentless power
of creation

**oh, and how you'll gasp
when you finally see it**

#16

being human
is very hard work

but my love,
I need you
to be kind with me
because

I am you

we are both the same little bursts of energy
controlling these skin and bone suits
as best as we can while we ride
together on this same spinning spaceship

be soft with me
because

I am you

we are both still trying to remember
the last thing the voice of Love sang
to us while we were taken out of
the same cradle of time and into life

be careful with me
because

I am you

we both have been intentionally and unintentionally wounded by people
who were frantically trying to win the same race that has no actual finish
line or trophy to hoist

be merciful with me
because

I am you

John Roedel

we have both intentionally and unintentionally
wounded others while attempting to follow
the same script that was written centuries ago
by people who were afraid

be present with me
because

I am you

we are both being constantly seduced by
the relentless guilt and anxiety who want us
who want us to be rooted in the same toxic soil
or the unchangeable past or the uncertain future

be sweet with me
because

I am you

we are both floating down the same
narrow lazy river that is carrying
us to the same endless ocean where we
will relearn how to surf on waves of eternity

be understanding me
because

I am you

we are both going to someday
be connected to one another again like bulbs
on the same string of lights where one glow blends effortlessly into the
next one

~be kind to me~
~be soft with me~
~be careful with me~
~be merciful with me~
~be present with me~
~be sweet with me~
~be compassionate with me~

oh, my love,
be so very human with me

John Roedel

Fitting In Is For Sardines 51

because because because
because because because
because

I am you

#17

For the past 22 years, my son has unknowingly recited this poem to me every day.

~ Autism doesn't mean broken

it means "Incandescent smile."
it means "Courage beyond measure."
it means "Watch this!"
it means "Don't you dare doubt me.
it means "This is a world of miracles."
it means "Different is beautiful."
it means "Hope endures."
it means " Unashamed!"
it means "My story is still to be written."

~ Autism doesn't mean broken

it means "Life is a flowerbed of countless unique colors."
it means "Burning heart."
it means "Love doesn't stop."
it means "I have dignity."
it means "I'm more than my diagnosis.
it means "I'm the Angel of joy."
it means "The art of living in the present moment."
it means "Raw honesty."

~ Autism doesn't mean broken

it means "Obstacles don't scare me."
it means "Let me teach you how to forgive."
it means "Sunflower in the desert."
it means "A living example of wonderment."
it means "The mastery of gratitude."
it means "My goodness can't be obscured."
it means "Whenever I face a wall I build a door."
it means "My life is a song."

~ Autism doesn't mean broken

John Roedel

it means "I shall not be judged."
it means "Happiness is the journey not the destination."
it means "Please don't give up on me."
it means "My light inside is just as bright as yours."
it means "I see souls."
it means "Be patient with me."
it means "I fight every day."
it means "Better get out of my way!"
it means "Nothing will stop me."
it means "I'm worthy."

~ *Autism doesn't mean broken*

it means "Created to be an instrument."
it means "Listen to my eyes."
it means "A stretching ripple of grace."
it means "Unafraid."
it means "Deserving of love."
it means "Patron Saint of the rising sun."
it means "Don't leave me behind."
it means "I'm still in here."
it means "Howling fearlessness."
it means "Let me show you how to change the world."

~ *Autism doesn't mean broken*

it means "Every breath is a gift."
it means "Proof of the human spirit."
it means "Open hands."
it means "Vessel of strength."
it means "Don't tell me what I can't do."
it means "Every second counts."
it means "Adventure."
it means "A psalm of the furious rejoice!"
it means "Kissed by heaven."
it means "Defying expectations."
it means "I will not be hidden!"

~ *Autism doesn't mean broken*

it means "Wild drum solo!"
it means "You don't have to understand me to love me."
it means "Honored Warrior."
it means "Daylight peeking through trees."
it means "Your expectations don't concern me."
it means "Mountain climber."

John Roedel

it means "Covered in blossoms."
it means "Eternal spring."
it means "I never met an enemy."
it means "Bet on me."

~ Autism doesn't mean broken

it means "My veins run with gold and fire."
it means "I can't wait to prove them wrong."
it means "Butterfly in a cocoon."
it means "Dance with me."
it means "I make my own paths!"
it means "I don't need your pity."
it means "A lighthouse on the shore of compassion."
it means "Let me tell you my dreams!"
it means "I walk through fire every damned day."
it means "Fear is no match for willpower"

~ Autism doesn't mean broken

it means "I will be your living poem."
it means "Just believe in me!"
it means "I can do anything."
it means "Don't be afraid of me."
it means "If you let me I can teach you peace."
it means "Yes, I matter."
it means "I keep getting back on my feet."
it means "The Sermon of Silver Linings."
it means "Nothing is wrong with me."
it means "Treasure hunter."
it means "Radiating zest!

autism means "My heart isn't a spilled-out puzzle - it's a mosaic of sacred stained glass painting the hardwood floors of this world with the divine light.

autism means "*Go ahead and sing - I'm going to play the holy hell out of these drums!*"

autism means

*I will always
find a light in the dark*

that is what autism is

John Roedel

#18

Me: Hey God.

God: Hello, My love.

Me: I think I'm supposed to go through that door.

God: Well, let's give it a go.

Me: I dunno. It looks kind of scary.

God: It's just a new opportunity. What's so scary about that?

Me: There could be something terrible on the other side of the door.

God: True. Although, there could also be something wonderful waiting for you.

Me: Hmm.

God: Let's shake things up. Open it. You can't spend your entire life just looking at doors without ever opening any of them. Aren't you curious?

Me: I'd rather be safe.

God: I think you've become addicted to safety.

Me: What's wrong with that?

God: I didn't create eagles to stay in their nests. I didn't sunlight to remain obscured behind the clouds. I didn't create the tide for people to just watch and not jump in.

Me: Um? What?

God: I didn't create you to settle for a lifetime of safety and comfort. I created you for adventure and exploration. I created you to walk through doors and thresholds so you can embrace new people and experiences.

John Roedel

Me: Ack! That sounds absolutely terrifying!

God: It will be - but sometimes a May flower must risk the frost if it wants to feel the June bloom. Open the door. See what is waiting for you.

Me: I'll think about it.

God: Quit stalling. The time is now.

Me: I can't. I'm too worried about what's on the other side.

God: You know what's on the other side?

Me: What's that?

God: *Everything.*

John Roedel

#19

For most of my life
I've treated doors like paintings
in a fancy museum.

~ I look, but never touch~

God surrounds me with
big fat doors but I keep
choosing to use
them as prison walls.

Doors are for people
who are going places.

That's never been me.

I haven't been going
anywhere for years.

I'm a stuck person.

A stuck person just looks at
doors until they turn
into coatracks.

There is dust gathering in my heart.
There are vines growing around my soul.

Today, I pray for the courage
to squeeze my hand on the doorknob
and open the door that's been waiting
for me to see what is on the other side.

Join me.

Shake off the dust.
Become unstuck.
Take a risk.

Open the door.

John Roedel

Sure,
we may get hurt
or
we may find treasure.

Whatever happens is better than
the terrible numbness of being stuck.

Turn your knob.
Open your door.

We aren't here for safety
We are here for adventure.

~ today is the last day we hide
behind doors ~

This is the age of crossing thresholds

~ and I can't wait to find you over there
on the other side of our fears.

I bet we laugh more.

love,
me

John Roedel

#20

someday, in your most insecure hour

~ when you feel like maybe your life
is some sort of a cosmic mistake

I want you to close your eyes

and imagine that you are holding
your newborn self in your arms

feel the heat of the baby's skin press up
against your present-day bare chest

notice how your two heartbeats
each take turns to keep the rhythm
between who the person were born
to be and the person who you are now

and if you listen to those dueling heartbeats
for long enough

you will hear a voice whispering to you
between each of your alternating palpitations

and you will immediately recognize it
as the Voice of Love that you heard
right before your soul light was painted
in flesh

notice how this whispering voice
is saying the same words over and
over on a loop

and somehow you will know that the voice
has been playing this message since the day you drew your first breath

it is saying:

"you are born of miracle

John Roedel

*to be a miracle
to someday return to miracle"*

my love,
in that moment
look down at your
neonatal form

while the voice reminds
you of your

*~worth
~dignity
~significance
~value
~goodness
~importance*

feel how the doubt you have
in yourself will start to
soften like butter sitting
in the sun

this plague of insecurity
has been preying on how exhausted
this modern world makes us all feel

but - it has one weakness:

our lives
(however we got here)
are a miracle

and if we try our best to honor
the marvel of our very existence

our insecurities will have
no choice but to let
go of our singing throats

~ no, it won't happen right away

but the more time you spend
with your newborn self

listening to the Voice of Love

John Roedel

speak to you through the grooves
of your dueling vinyl hearts

you will remember
how important your life is

and what a wonder child
of creation you have always been

John Roedel

#21

this isn't how I planned for
my life to look like," I whispered
under my breath as I walked to my car

"tell me about it,"
an eavesdropping cloud
replied to me from above

I looked up and watched
the cloud billow between looking
like a dove and an open hand

the cloud continued:

*"I used to be a snowfield in Montana.
I used to be a dewdrop kiss on a lily.
I used to be a puddle in a parking lot.
I used to be a river in Mexico.
I used to be a glacier.
I used to be a waterfall mist in a jungle.*

I used to be so many things."

"doesn't that make you sad?" I asked the cloud

"it used to - but not anymore," the cloud replied while wrapping herself around me like a scarf. "I don't think either of us were created to stay the same form our entire life."

"I'm not sure I can let go of my old life," I sighed.

"oh you simply must," the cloud whispered in my ear.
" because once you release what you used to be
and embrace who you are meant to be now -
something amazing will happen," the cloud said

"what's that?" I asked while looking at my hands which were beginning to billow and shapeshift.

John Roedel

"you'll start to float."

and with that, my feet lifted off the ground

#22

Someday we won't ask our children:

"What do you want
to be when you grow up."

The question we will ask instead will be:

"What kind of miracle
are you going to be?"

And the world will be
better off for it.

When I was a kid I was never asked what I wanted to be when I became an adult.

Nobody knew what to do with me.
Not my teachers.
Not my parents.

~ Not even me.

Maybe no one ever thought I would actually grow up, so there was no point of trying to figure it out.

Now that I'm older -

and I'm a bit untethered.
and I'm drifting a little
and I'm sort of aimless

it turns out that

my greatest professional ambition is to someday have my a row of shamrocks named after me.

Other than that goal
I'm just wandering.

John Roedel

~ Wait no, I'm not wandering.

Wandering isn't a strong enough
word for what has become of me.

I became profoundly lost.

I never get
anywhere.

And

I never became
anything.

Now that I'm older, untethered, drifting, lost and never got anywhere or became anything - I'm so very tempted to badger my children into worrying about WHAT they are going to be in twenty years.

I know that is what I'm supposed to do.

Fretting about what job kids will have is a major part of the script parents are given to memorize.

I'm meant to grey myself over my children's college exam scores and bloviate at them for blowing a history quiz - because how in the hell are they ever going to become a corporate lawyer if they don't know every detail of what happened during the War of 1812?!

I think I'm meant to fret
and yell at them more.

But I just can't.

I'm more worried about who they are going to be all the time, rather than what they are going to be doing for 8-hours a day when they are in their mid-thirties.

If forced to choose, I'd rather have my sons live their life as a pauper who is covered in perspective and kindness than an asshole dermatologist who snaps at his waiter and forgets that their life is just a speck of dust living on a bigger speck of dust that is flying through an expanding universe that appears to have no end.

The hope is that they land somewhere in between those two options.

John Roedel

There is an elusive intersection where both joy and material success meet. I've never found it for myself - but I will leave them a map made of poetry written on a coffeehouse napkin that should help them begin their search for that sweet elusive spot.

As a father of three boys, I will mark my grade as a parent by

how generous they become
and by how they treat others
and by how seriously they won't take themselves
and by how much laughter they spread
and by how they give their hearts to people
and by how authentically they live their lives.

I know that all of that makes me sound like a hands-off parent. Let me try and earn back some credibility with you.

I want my kids to value their service to the world more than they do their 401Ks or which all-inclusive resort they will visit next.

Someday when my children are gathered around my gravestone I pray that they will hold up a caramel-colored glass of Irish whiskey and toast their unsuccessful father who never became something but always worked so hard to be somebody.

There is a difference between the two things.

Kids,
Don't be something.
Be somebody.

Somebody who is kind
Somebody who is merciful
Somebody who is unaffected by the expectations of other people.

Somebody who believed in
miracles so deeply
that they became one themself.

Kids,
just be yourselves.

I mean it.

Be authentically you.

John Roedel

You each have
a body that under its skin wrapping
has a caldera of endless light

- that once it breaks through
-will shoot forth an
arc of light that can
be seen from Venus.

Don't be something.

Be more than that.

~ Be the miracle this
world needs right now.

Be you.

Locate the intersection
of joy and success.

When you find it, please plant a
row of shamrocks nearby
and name it after me.

John Roedel

#23

On days like today,
when my eyesight is failing
and my bones ache more than usual

I have to
remember that

I am not my body

it is simply just the
Airbnb that I am renting

my Wyoming wind-whipped dry skin
and my graying hair is just
the package I was
vacuumed sealed inside of

my love,

there is so much
more to us than our
neurons and nerves

we are timeless
tourists on a tour
straight into the mystical

we are

pieces of cosmic energy
caught inside this temporary jar
of humming organs and flowing veins

we are miracle sparks that were launched
out of the First Fire eons ago who eventually
were given starships of our own to command that
were built out of muscle and membranes

my love,

John Roedel

these gangly skeletons
we are lugging around
are the jungle gym cradle
for our playful souls

but these physical forms
aren't who we are
any more than the hull or the sail
we are steering

these human containers
are just the vessels
taking us on adventure
after adventure

until someday
angels in sailor hats
come and decommission
our flesh and blood

my love,

~ do not fear that day
when we shed our skin

because

we are the energy
who existed long
before our freckles
started frecking

remember

you are the glimmering precious cargo
inside this built-to-fail body

and someday

when you have to turn it all back in
to the eternal rental agency

you'll finally get to stretch your celestial wings
and join the rest of us fireflies out here at the edge of time

where the Great Artist is still painting worlds

John Roedel

for us to someday explore

my love,

you are not our body

you are the supernatural
miracle bouncing around
inside of it

> *my love,*
>
> *you are the
> endless fire*

#24

my love,
here is my unsolicited
Valentine's Day wish for you

quit waiting
for someone else

to finally love you
the way that
you deserve
to be loved

you only
get so much
time here

quit wasting it
on people who
can't recognize
a masterpiece of
creation when it's
standing right in front
of them

you only get
so many spins
on this planet

quit squandering the ride
on people who fail to see
the breadcrumb trail to the cosmos
in your eyes

my love,
in case you were still wondering:

~ you are a once-in-a-million-year wonder

and it's past time
for you to only

John Roedel

Fitting In Is For Sardines 72

spend your days
with people who need
to catch their breath
whenever you walk
into a room

my love,
if someone
doesn't hold
you like a precious
gemstone

they aren't worthy
of feeling the heat of
your reflecting light
against their skin

you are the rarest
treasure existence
has ever known

and if they don't
tremble when they
touch you

they aren't
the one

oh, my love,
please remember

you are a
Rembrandt
in a sundress

whose image burns
itself on the inside
of our eyelids

you are a miracle
of grace and fire
that angels
play trumpets for

you are the first
watermelon of the summer

John Roedel

~sweet
~light
~soul-quenching

don't you dare
let anyone else
treat you any less
than the marvel
you were so carefully
designed to be

John Roedel

#25

I had been in an arranged marriage
with all of the expectations the world
had for me

it took all my strength
to find enough courage to
to break up with the dreams
other people had dreamt for me

and I left the fiancé of
their predictions for my life

at the altar

and I eloped with my authentic self
straight into the uncharted lands of

"Who the hell knows what
comes next but it will all
be quite a wild romp!"

I let go of what was
expected of me and now
I'm holding onto my heart
for dear life as the two of us
ride off into the horizon
    of my divine purpose

my love,
come join me

out here in the beautiful chaos
of getting to decide for yourself
what your own life will look like

become a runaway bride
with your comet trail wedding dress
shooting rainbow sparks as you disappear
straight up into the fading night sky

John Roedel

become a groom who strips out of the
tuxedo you were given at 18 for
the comfortable birthday suit
denim jeans of your true naked self

come meet me out here on the tip
of Creation's paintbrush where
every dripping color is brand new
and unique

- just like you

my love,
you didn't escape the cold void
just to tie the knot with the ordinary

you made it all the way here to discover,
fall in love with, and then marry the soulmate
who was designed for you with
the utmost of care: ~ *yourself*

don't make a lifelong commitment
to a snoozy existence that isn't your own

give yourself to the untamed oul who had
been sitting right under your nose this whole time

and someday

you will have such
a love story to tell

John Roedel

#26

My love,

*Start to treat your body
Like it's a hospice bed*

As if it were a sacred dwelling

*That will someday become
The cocoon*

*Where you rest as
You figure out what you need*

To become next

John Roedel

#27

Recently, the lady across from me in a waiting room asked me if I was ready for things to "get back to normal"

I smiled and shook my head

"I wasn't very good at normal," I told her.
"I'd like the give weird a bit of a try."

She blinked.
I blinked back.

things had gotten awkward
~ I always make things awkward ~

She blinked again.
I responded with another blink.

We were now communicating
through eyelash morse code.

So I blinked the following message to her:

I'm not waiting for things
to go back to normal

things are already
way too ordinary for me
to wish for it to have
any more of a hold over me

to be honest,
I'm waiting for things
to become more abnormal

normal had its time as the DJ
normal played the same songs over and over

typical's reign as the queen has gone on for so long
that her crown has begun to grow into her skin

John Roedel

Fitting In Is For Sardines 78

I know you can sense it, too

this cocoon we are living in
is starting to quiver and our
skin is starting to turn into
polka-dotted butterfly wings

we are all unraveling
in the most beautiful ways

can't you feel it in your veins?

your plain blood is bleeding
itself into the sharpest pattern

of flowing plaid

you have shifted like a Corvette
on an empty coastline highway at sunset

you can feel the hum deep
inside the transmission of your soul

your engine is growling with the
power of one billion angelic horses

you are now able to go from the natural
to the supernatural in under 3 seconds

you are racing toward your raw purpose
you are speeding toward your wild dream

you are no longer a bore - you are a blur

I know you can feel it, too
you are as sick as I am about pretending that
all we want is for things to be normal

normal had its age
let's give the unusual an epoch or two

this is the season
of change and

your eyes are turning
Into a sponge

John Roedel

soaking up
every beautiful
oddity you see

and every now and
then when your
eyes have absorbed
just enough peculiar
artwork of the divine

they begin to pour
with tears of joy

I know you can feel it

nothing is going back
to the way things used to be

because our existence is a living
piece of clay being constantly molded
under the loving hands of a cosmic potter

normal doesn't live
here anymore

it's been replaced
with the abjectly strange

and isn't that how it should be?

every day we should wake up ready
to journey into the wonderfully irregular

this is the age for you
to finally embrace
the eccentric and exotic

which is perfect
because that is exactly what you are

eccentric & exotic

there is nothing like you
among the uncountable stars

John Roedel

you are the rarest precious gemstone

you know it
~ you can feel it

right under your scars
right behind your eyes
right inside of your heart

is a river of light
that had never existed before
you were created

you are profoundly and beautifully
abnormal

and that is why this age
is perfect for you

normal is on the outs
atypical is in

and you, my wild love,
are the loveliest
deviation from the norm
that has ever drawn a breath

and this is your time
and you are about to change the world

and I can't wait to watch

John Roedel

#28

to love those who despise us
we must become like rainclouds
over the desert

we must pour our compassion
out even if it means it will
evaporate long before it reaches
the ground

because even a single drop of
our love hitting the cracked surface
can spark a revolution of
badland wildflowers

rain your love on those who
hate you without any concern
if it gets there or not

and maybe someday
your foe will show up
at your door with a bouquet
of desert willows in their hand
for you to replant in your garden

my love,

reconciliation is a
quivering cloudburst

and everyone deserves a sunshower of your charity
- even your enemy

-and especially if your enemy is you

I can smell the clemency in the air,
can't you?

I can feel the joyful ache
of reunion in my bones,
can't you

John Roedel

Fitting In Is For Sardines 82

                                                                                     it's building
on the once-dry horizon

mercy rain
mercy rain
mercy rain

John Roedel

#29

*I can't think of
anything more
boring*

*than living by
the expectations
of other people*

*let the hens gossip
and cluck and clack
whenever you walk
into the room with your
mismatched socks and
stardust falling out
of your wild pink hair*

*because in a little while
when you get up to leave
to continue on with
your adventure*

*every single one of them
will secretly wish that
they were going with you*

John Roedel

#30

if you don't like
the way that you
look it's probably
because you have
chosen the wrong
mirror to look at
yourself in

stop using other people as a mirror
to see your reflection in

- *especially if that other person is unkind*

unkind people make the worst mirrors
they only want to reflect back your blemishes

and your weaknesses
and your fault lines
and your sins

don't blame them for making you feel bad
you are the one looking for them
to tell you how you look

of course, they will tell you that you're ugly
of course, they will say you aren't enough

they are unkind- what did you expect?

while we are at it...
you should also
stop using your
bank account as a mirror

it's a liar

money doesn't reflect
you who you really are

          neither does your car
            or your grades

              John Roedel

> or your awards
> or your Instagram
> or your past mistakes
> or your diagnosis
> or your late bills
> or your failures

none of those things make very good mirrors

If you want to know how you actually look I suggest that you hold a baby for a bit.

Pay attention to how a baby will look at you. To a baby, you are a garden of a million glowing pastel moon flowers. You are a wonder. You are exotic.

To a baby, you are a giant. You are an ancient warrior protecting them from monsters and uncomfortable rashes. You fill up their sky like a brilliant supernova. You are the sky and sea.

To a baby laying in your arms, you are both the cradle and the lullaby. A baby will gaze at you with wide eyes and an uncontrollable smile because they have just come from heaven and they know divinely crafted beauty when they see it.

They see the miracle in you. They see the miracle in you. They see the miracle in you.

Babies make the best mirrors. Look at your reflection the EXACT way a baby looks at you.

For too long you have let dirty and broken shards of glass tell you who you are.

Those reflections are corrupt - stop trusting them.

Let the innocent show you who you are. They see your light. They see you for who you are:

> *Capable*
> *Strong*
> *Beautiful*
> *Burning*
> *Blooming*
> *Becoming*

John Roedel

#31

whenever I feel helpless
in this overwhelming world

I become a helper

oh, oh,
my love

on the days
when it feels like
I have no power

I serve others

you see,
whenever I wash
the world's feet

my hands
immediately
stop shaking

~ and I find peace
~ and I reclaim my power
~ and I get back to work

John Roedel

#32

Me: Hey God.

God: Hey there, My Love.

Me: Help me fit in.

God:

Me: Help me be normal.

God:

Me: Help Me be just like everyone else.

God:

Me: Help me live my life exactly how people expect me to.

God:

Me: *Help me shine!!*

God: **I THOUGHT YOU WOULD NEVER ASK!!!!**

John Roedel

#33

1) it's not selfish
to be kind to
yourself

2) it's not selfish
to be kind to
yourself

3) it's not selfish
to be kind to
yourself

~ needless guilt is like quicksand;
be careful how long you stand in it ~

1) it's okay to question
something you were
once certain of

2) it's okay to question
something you were
once certain of

3) it's okay to question
something you were
once certain of

~ doubt will lead you off the map to explore the most
beautiful untouched places in your heart ~

1) you will never be
ashamed of your
tears again

2) you will never be
ashamed of your
tears again

3) you will never be
ashamed of your

John Roedel

Fitting In Is For Sardines 89

tears again

~ your lovely flushed red cheeks glow
with the courage of raw authenticity ~

1) other people's expectations of
you will not be the narrator
of your story

2) other people's expectations of
you will not be the narrator
of your story

3) other people's expectations of
you will not be the narrator
of your story

~ the only voice you will ever follow
will come from within ~

1) rock bottom will never become
a dungeon for you - it will will
always be your secret temple

2) rock bottom will never become
a dungeon for you - it will will
always be your secret temple

3) rock bottom will never become
a dungeon for you - it will will
always be your secret temple

~ God is helping you scratch out your
comeback plans on the cavern walls ~

1) you are a breathtaking piece
of mysterious artwork that
was crafted by the Divine

2) you are a breathtaking piece
of mysterious artwork that
was crafted by the Divine

3) you are a breathtaking piece
of mysterious artwork that
was crafted by the Divine

John Roedel

Fitting In Is For Sardines 90

~ I can still smell the cosmic wet clay
on the grooves of your heart ~

1) you won't
give up
today

2) you won't
give up
today

3) you won't
give up
today

~ the world still needs to hear your sweet song;
I still need to feel your hands wrapped in mine ~

1) this is where
you come
back to life

2) this is where
you come
back to life

3) this is where
you come
back to life

~ and I can't wait to watch your bare-skinned
scars teach me how to heal under the moonlight ~

(the power of 3)

John Roedel

#34

~when they hate you
for having the courage
to be yourself

you may be tempted to stop
being the person you were created to be

~when they hate you
for the shape, difference, gender
or the color of your body

you may feel compelled to turn the rolling boil
of your intensity into a mild simmer

you may try to escape their hate
by conforming to it

you might just want to
bury your burning light under a thick canopy
of their reckless judgment

~don't
~you
~dare

my love,

while you weren't looking
you became a hero to so many
of us who wish we could live as
unapologetically as you do

I watched you just being yourself
and it gave me the bravery
to start speaking in my own voice

you can't stop now

the hate that they lay
on your doorstep is

John Roedel

a sign that you are
getting to them

the cruelty they plaster
on the walls is a sign
that you are scaring them
by simply being the person you
we're born to be

if they don't like you
then they should take
it up with God

you are just being you

~*lovely you*
courageous you

~*fierce you*
divine you

~*audacious you*

don't back down

not in the face
of such hate

the angrier they get
at you for living your
life authentically

~the more beautiful you get
the more you glow
~the more lost ones you save
the more anointed you become

remember, you are
the lighthouse guiding
us back home

I'm following your light
I'm coming to the shore
I'm crawling through the surf
I'm standing right next to you now

John Roedel

if they hate you
they can hate me too

this isn't your fight
it's ours together

and I sure do like our chances

#35

When I feel empty inside
         (like I do today)

I pretend I'm a newborn universe
waiting for a single spark to ignite
the boiler of creation and kick off a
new age inside of me

I imagine this painful emptiness I feel is exactly what a patch of untouched soil feels like before a wildflower seed begins to shake and stretch out from under the blanket of dirt

~ *emptiness used to scare me*

I always assumed this empty void
that lingers in my heart was proof
that I had been abandoned by God

~ *I don't see it that way anymore*

these days my emptiness means
I remain wonderfully unfinished

even though I haven't had my big bang yet
but I can feel it so close to happening
that I can see traces of light forming out
of the canvas of nothingness in front of me

isn't that the benefit of being
so used to the dark?

that any trickle of light can appear
like a new sun

I haven't grown my garden yet
but the flowers scratching
on the topsoil

and the petals of these exotic

John Roedel

petals are swirling under
the peat moss of my life

so, now when I feel that
empty feeling, my love,

I don't give into despair

I feel excited about what's to come
and instead of surrendering
to the dark night

instead,
I surrender to hope

And when I do,

I can feel a dozen butterflies
dancing around inside of me looking for
walls to bump into

I know it sounds crazy
but the emptiness has often
created a frenzied swarm inside of me

and I always feel like
I have given the butterflies
a brief welcome message:

"Oh sweet butterflies,
you will find no walls
or fences in me

~ just an endless expanse

so, enjoy the space to roam!"

And maybe that is why
I feel so unfilled inside
sometimes

because I've left so much room for hope to
finally build her kingdom inside of me

I know it sounds unhinged

John Roedel

but...

does the sky feel empty
without any clouds or birds
in it?

no -it just keeps stretching its horizon
to visit places it has never been before

and that is just like our hearts

*they are more sky
then they are cathedrals*

*they are more untamed expanse
then they are an ornate hotel*

our hearts are built
without borders
or limits

oh, my love,
we don't give into
the emptiness

we let it remind us to keep inviting
hope to come and grow a new world
and endless sprawling garden inside of us

*come hope
come hope
come hope*

I am completely vacant
I am a blank canvas
I am an unplayed note

*come hope
come hope
come hope*

dear hope,
build your
kingdom in me

you will that

John Roedel

there is plenty of
interior space
for you to renovate

just mind all of the
wildly dancing butterflies

who all seem to be
having a most fabulous time"

John Roedel

#36

*people aren't
born broken*

that's not how
any of this works

~ every single
one of us is born
a song that nobody
has ever heard before

~ every single
one of us is born
a teacher that will help
remind the world
life is precious and dignified

~ everyone single
one of us is born
a miracle that proves
there is magic in
every heartbeat

I didn't know what true bravery
was until I watched my son
turn his autism into a
treasure hunting adventure

~he has fought the dragons in his mind
and explored the dungeon of prejudice

and endured the orcs
who were hell-bent on setting
fire to the blood in his veins

~ he experienced all of those terrifying things
only to discover that

**he was
the treasure**

John Roedel

*that he was
searching
for the
entire time*

the valor I've seen from people living
with a disability is the only proof I need that
there is no shame in being unique

different isn't broken

different is beautiful
different is bravery
different is boundless

~different is unbroken

God, may I be
a better witness to
these disciples
of courage

who each day wear their differences
with untamed pride and sly knowing smiles

because they remembered
something that most of us
have forgotten long ago

they remembered:

that all life is a gift
~and all life is precious
~and that each life is a miracle

every single one

John Roedel

#37

I love dancing
because I'm
so fearlessly
terrible at it

I have zero natural
rhythm but that never
stops me from moving
my rump in such
a gawky manner
that would indicate to
anybody watching
from a distance that
I likely just sat on
an active beehive

my dancing is a casserole
of wild pelvic thrusts
and pouring sweat that
feature a healthy amount of

~ *Reckless Floundering*

with a dash of

~ *Untamed Folly*

and a couple of sprinkles of

~ *Sweet Prancing Flubber*

I've been told by esteemed
mystics that my dancing
has been known to be
so untamed and wild that
it tears open the thin
veil that separates us
from the spirit world

my movements are said
to be so unhinged that
it invites the ghosts

John Roedel

Fitting In Is For Sardines 101

that only I can see
to put on their
astral ballroom shoes
and to dance with me
until we all fade into the
first light spilling over
predawn sky like it
is celestial milk

~ my salsa is anything but mild

~my samba will make you cry to your mama

~my hustle is proof that the laws of physics can be bent

~ my jive is an element of slow-motion magic and sweat

there is no bad day
that a deep pounding bass
and a little space for me to spin
my boogie-woogie
around like it's cotton candy
can't cure

~ you can have your Roomba
I'll take my Rumba

~ you can visit Nova Scotia
I'm vacationing in Bossa Nova

~ while you are sleeping your eight hours
I'll be waltzing under a waxing moon

~ your bar hopping
will never trump my lindy hopping

my smile is at its stretchiest
the more I move my feet
and shake my middle-aged ass

dancing takes my
natural introversion
and buries it under
the dance floor

I spend my days parsing

John Roedel

Fitting In Is For Sardines

my words and guarding my
thoughts like they are the queen

but when I'm dancing

~oh, when I'm dancing

there is nobody watching the door
there is no splitting hairs
there is not a single moment of hesitation

*it's all pop
and no-can stop*

*it's all shag
and no drag*

*it's all groove
with nothing to prove*

I live my non-dancing life
so cautiously

I constantly hear the voice in my ear:

"careful where you step, John,
don't land on anybody's toes

look where you're going
what will people think, John?

don't do anything to draw attention
take a break, John,

you're a punchline, John,
go sit down, John,

you're embarrassing yourself"

but when I'm dancing

~ oh, but when I'm dancing...

the music
and my heartbeat
evict those lies

John Roedel

Fitting In Is For Sardines 103

from my head

I become a late-day thunderstorm
of booming feet and lighting gyrations

I am an
insatiable whirl

~ a blur of short legs and ravenous eyes

without a single care given
about what You r I think

because there is no thinking
when I dance

there is just constant movement

~ it's unrehearsed joy

it's a celebration of raw carelessness
it's the public display of my knots being untied

**I wish I lived
like I danced**

unashamed for how bad I am at it
unafraid of your judgment
unwilling to let a single misstep to slow me down

unburdened by any
concern for my past or future

and so very unstoppable

why is it that the older we get
the less we dance?

it seems like it should
be the opposite

I want my gray hair to
become the disco ball
I boogie under

oh God,

John Roedel

*as my skin
becomes thinner
and my veins become
bluer let my body turn
into a blaring
gospel of moving wonder*

oh God,

*keep the music
blasting on the dance
floor of my heart*

oh God,

*let my children
know me more for
my terrible dancing
and less for my
masterful worrying*

oh God,

*let me be
more like Bacon
and less like Lithgow*

oh God,

*let my life
become an unpracticed
two-step that keeps starting
me on an adventure of infinite wonder*

oh God,

*there better
be dancing in
heaven*

because I'm bringing
the moves with me that
will make even Your
most devout
angels blush

John Roedel

#38
Dear kids,

I have nine things on my heart
that I need to say to you before
the sun sets

ONE

the people
who come to
steal your wonder
are the same
folks who
long ago let
others freely
take theirs

never let it
go

it's yours

cling to
your sweetness
and become a
living witness to
the million
beautiful curiosities
of your life

don't let anything
become mundane

I'm serious

pay close attention
to the adventure
before you

all of your experiences
are soaked in magic

John Roedel

the good and the bad
the happy and the sad
the hilarious and the mad

some people will
want you to treat your
pulse like it's boring

it's anything but

your life is bathed
in stardust

I know that doesn't
make much sense now
but I'll explain that a bit
later

TWO

every time you
see a mother
holding her baby
I want you to
fall down the
rabbit hole of
of creation's divine
mastery
babies are the
key to the mystery
of our entire experience here
don't let a baby pass by
you without becoming bewildered by
the whole wonderful oddity of life

THREE

during the times
when your stomach
hurts from laughing
so much with your soul friend

I need you to not let
the moment slip past
you without first

John Roedel

acknowledging the unappreciated
miracle of your deepest relationship

the soul friends that you meet
here on Earth are the same ones
that you knew before you came
into being

you knew each other before birth
and promised to find one another
down here in the blood and mud
good work you two!

FOUR

when your heart
gets broken

- and it will -

I am begging you
to count each tear
that rolls down your
face as the blessing
that it is
you are crying
because you haven't
let your heart go numb

you are crying
because you let
yourself be vulnerable

you are crying
because you are
still fighting to stay alive

you are crying
because you have
accepted your humanity

every tear
is proof of how
incredibly strong
you are

John Roedel

be proud of your shedding tears!

each tear is unique
telling your story
drop by beautiful drop

FIVE

on the occasion
when you find
yourself watching
a juicy sunset, please
spend a fat second
breathing in the last
seconds of the dying light

take a moment to
learn the great lesson of twilight:

despite the long night
the light always returns

darkness always loses
the game is rigged

SIX

someday you will be
kissed tenderly
by a person who recognizes
the treasure in you

don't you dear treat
it like anything other
then the strange marvel that it is

if you let any of your kisses
become ordinary than
everything else in your life
will quickly follow

SEVEN

every breath you take
is proof that your

John Roedel

existence is a singular event

there will never be anybody
else like you again

everything you do
makes history

every time you exhale
it sends a fresh ripple
through the galaxy

listen,

there is only
one you

every second that washes
over you is something
brand new that this universe
has never seen before

be fearless

EIGHT

someday we will hold
hands for the last time

but if you let that
moment take root
inside of you it
will last a thousand
lifetimes

let our fleeting time
together grow into a
towering redwood tree

time is relentless

but it is no match for
love

honor every second
of the clock

John Roedel

treat every little
bit of your experience
like the wild phenomenon
that it is

be a vigilant witness
to the magic of
everything

NINE

*don't become forgetful
of your dignity*

or that on the day
each of you were born
you were covered in
the dust of first-day creation

you were forged
out of the most brilliant
of celestial fires

never take for
granted all of
that radiates in
you

*you were born
to blaze*

*don't forget
don't forget
don't forget*

John Roedel

#39

Me: Hey God.

God: Hello, My love.

Me: I'm falling apart. Can you put me back together?

God: I would rather not.

Me: Why?

God: Because you aren't a puzzle.

Me: What about all the pieces of my life that are falling onto the ground?

God: Let them stay there for a while. They fell off for a reason. Take some time and decide if you need any of those pieces back.

Me: You don't understand! I'm breaking down!

God: No - you don't understand. You are breaking through. What you are feeling are just growing pains. You are shedding the things and the people in your life that are holding you back. You aren't falling apart. You are falling into place. Relax. Take some deep breaths and allow those things you don't need anymore to fall off of you. Quit holding onto the pieces that don't fit you anymore. Let them fall off. Let them go.

Me: Once I start doing that, what will be left of me?

God: Only the very best pieces of you.

Me: I'm scared of changing.

God: I keep telling you - YOU AREN'T CHANGING!! YOU ARE BECOMING!

Me: Becoming who?

God: Becoming who I created you to be! A person of light and love and charity and hope and courage and joy and mercy and grace and compassion. I made you for more than the shallow pieces you have decided to adorn yourself with that you cling to with such greed and fear.

John Roedel

Let those things fall off of you. I love you! Don't change! Become! Become! Become! Become who I made you to be. I'm going to keep telling you this until you remember it.

Me: There goes another piece.

God: Yep. Let it be.

Me: So...I'm not broken?

God: *No - but you are breaking like the dawn. It's a new day. Become!! Become!!*

John Roedel

#40

it is so exhausting
pretending to be
somebody else

just to make other
people feel comfortable

I've found that the
disguises we force
each other to wear
are always so heavy

and they
often cause
slouching

my love,

when we allow
ourselves to glow
as we were intended

~ *we will never dim*

because unashamed
authenticity is
the most powerful
form of renewable
energy the universe
has ever known

blaze unafraid
blaze unafraid

my love,
blaze unafraid

John Roedel

Epilogue & Postscript

If I had a time machine

I would only go back to
change one thing in my childhood

I would sneak into
my 16-year old bedroom
and install stained glass
In my big window

so before mental illness
would come to shatter
me a couple of years layer

I would have already seen
how something can still
reflect the most beautiful light
long after they were so very broken

and then I wouldn't have felt like
I was ruined

because I would have already
embraced being a cosmic piece
of uneven art

by living under the glow of
stained glass

I wouldn't have been so afraid
of the eventual arrival my blueheart

because I would have already known
that despite how cracked I felt
my heart was still reflecting light

oh, if I had a time machine

I'd make sure I grew up

John Roedel

under the most lovely of
fractured light

*~ because that's all I
have ever wanted to be*

for everyone else

About The Author

John Roedel is an improv comedic who "stumbled" into writing a few years ago as his life began to fall apart all around him. During his dark night of the soul, John began to have fake conversations with "God" on Facebook to poke fun at his spiritual and personal crisis.

What began as a flippant way of making light of his doubts in the Divine turned into something he wasn't at all prepared for: God wrote back.

Since creating the popular "Hey God. Hey John." blog on Facebook three years ago, John has tackled such topics as his journey to mental health wellness, his lack of faith, the joy and pain of raising a child with autism, and grief, all in the form of a simple conversation with "God."

Eventually, these conversations transformed into poetry that has touched millions of people all around the world.

John's last two poetry collections book "Remedy" and "Upon Departure" were both Amazon bestsellers for poetry.

For more information on John Roedel please visit his website at johnroedel.com

John Roedel

Made in the USA
Las Vegas, NV
27 July 2023

75323720R00066